HOUGHTON MIFFLIN HARCOURT

JOURNEYS

Program Authors

James F. Baumann · David J. Chard · Jamal Cooks
J. David Cooper · Russell Gersten · Marjorie Lipson
Lesley Mandel Morrow · John J. Pikulski · Héctor H. Rivera
Mabel Rivera · Shane Templeton · Sheila W. Valencia
Catherine Valentino · MaryEllen Vogt

Consulting Author

Irene Fountas

HOUGHTON MIFFLIN HARCOURT
School Publishers

Cover illustration by Bernard Adnet.

Printed in the U.S.A.

ISBN 10:   0-54-725171-8
ISBN 13:   978-0-54-725171-4

3456789 - 0868 – 18 17 16 15 14 13 12 11 10
4500232057

Hello, Reader!

This book is full of characters who have something to share. A talented aunt shares her music, a thoughtful chipmunk makes something special for each of his friends, and an author shares a story about a lovable hat-wearing cat.

Turn the page to see what the authors of these stories have to share with you!

Sincerely,

The Authors

Sharing Time

Big Idea We all have something to share.

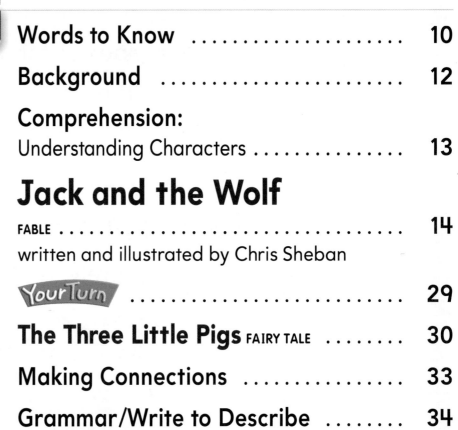

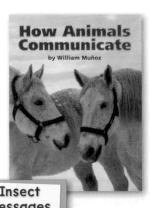

6

Sharing Time

Unit 2

Big Idea

We all have something to share.

Paired Selections

Read Together

✔ **WORDS TO KNOW**
HIGH-FREQUENCY WORDS

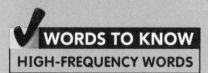

come
said
call
hear
away
every

Vocabulary
Reader

Context
Cards

Words to Know

● Read each Context Card.

● Choose two blue words.
Use them in sentences.

1

come

Wolf cubs come out of their den in the spring.

2

said

The ranger said that the cubs love to play.

3 call

A mother wolf can call to her cubs.

4 hear

Wolves hear better than people.

5 away

Wolves can travel far away from home.

6 every

Every wolf helps other wolves in its pack.

Background

✔ **WORDS TO KNOW**   **Sheep and Wolves**

1. Wolves hear sheep.

2. The wolves come to the field.

3. A man looks out for every sheep.

4. He will call the sheep to him.

5. He chases the wolves away.

6. "The sheep are safe!" the man said.

How does the man look out for the sheep?
How would you look out for the sheep?

12

Comprehension

✓ **TARGET SKILL** Understanding Characters

Characters are the people and animals in a story. Good readers think about what characters say and do. These are clues that show how characters feel and why they act as they do. Here is the character **Jack** from the next story.

Jack

As you read **Jack and the Wolf**, think about what Jack is like. Use a chart to write what he says and does.

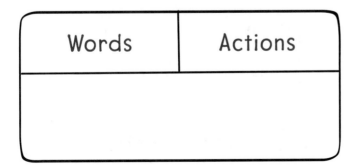

Words	Actions

✔ **WORDS TO KNOW**

come	hear
said	away
call	every

✔ **TARGET SKILL**

Understanding Characters Tell more about the characters.

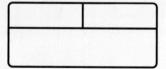

✔ **TARGET STRATEGY**

Summarize Stop to tell about main events.

GENRE

A **fable** is a short story that teaches a lesson. It may begin with **Once upon a time**.

Meet the Author and Illustrator

Chris Sheban

To create his artwork, Chris Sheban often uses watercolors and colored pencils. He has illustrated children's books and postage stamps. He joined with Tedd Arnold, Jerry Pinkney, and other artists to make the book **Why Did the Chicken Cross the Road?**

Jack and the Wolf

written and illustrated
by Chris Sheban

Essential Question

What lessons can you learn from story characters?

Once upon a time,
Jack sat on a big hill.

Jack had every sheep with him.
"It is not fun to sit," said Jack.

"I will yell **Wolf** for fun!"

His friends ran up the hill to help.
They did not see Wolf.

Jack sat back on the hill.
I will yell **Wolf**!

His friends ran back up the hill.
They did not see Wolf.

Jack sat back on the hill.

Wolf got up on a rock!

Jack and his sheep ran away.

"Did you hear me call?" said Jack.
"You did not come."

"You cannot trick us," said Nell.

"I will be good," said Jack.
"I will not trick you."

 **Cry Wolf**

Act It Out Act out **Jack and the Wolf** with a small group. Decide who will play Jack, the wolf, the sheep, and the villagers. You can add your own words. Show how the characters feel. SMALL GROUP

Turn and Talk — **Learning A Lesson**

Read the last page of the story again with a partner. Talk about the lesson Jack learned. Tell if you think he will change. Explain why you think so. UNDERSTANDING CHARACTERS

Connect to Traditional Tales

✔ **WORDS TO KNOW**

come	hear
said	away
call	every

GENRE

A **fairy tale** is a story with characters that can do amazing things.

TEXT FOCUS

A **storytelling phrase** often used at the end of fairy tales is **happily ever after.** Find this phrase in a sentence. What does it mean?

THE THREE LITTLE PIGS

Once upon a time there were three little pigs.

The first pig made a straw house. Soon he could hear Wolf call out.

"Let me come in," said Wolf.

"No," said the pig.
"I'll huff and I'll puff. I'll blow
your house in," Wolf said.

The second pig made a stick house.
"Let me come in," said Wolf.
"No," said the pig.

"I'll huff and I'll puff. I'll blow
your house in," Wolf said.

The third pig got bricks. He used
every brick to make a strong house.
Wolf could not blow this house in.
Wolf gave up and ran away.
The three pigs lived happily ever after.

Making Connections

 Text to Self

Retell a Story Why were the words **once upon a time** used in **Jack and the Wolf**? Retell this story to a classmate. Begin with **once upon a time**.

 Text to Text

Connect to Language Arts
Both stories tell about wolves. Tell how the wolf characters are alike and different.

Wolf Tales

 Text to World

Write to Explain Think about the lesson Jack learns. Write about a time you made a mistake. Tell what you learned.

Grammar

Read Together

Complete Sentences A **sentence** is a group of words. A sentence tells who or what. It also tells what someone or something does or did.

Sentence	Not a Sentence
Jan sits on a hill.	sits on a hill
Some sheep eat.	some sheep
One sheep ran away.	ran away

34

Find three word groups that are sentences.
Write them on another sheet of paper.
Then talk with a partner. Tell how you know
which word groups are sentences.

1. Ryan watches his sheep.

2. His dog helps him.

3. keeps the sheep safe

4. a few white sheep

5. A man cuts off their wool.

Grammar in Writing

When you proofread your writing, be sure
you have written complete sentences.

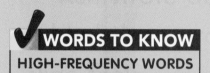

How Animals Communicate by William Muñoz

Insect Messages

✔ **WORDS TO KNOW**
HIGH-FREQUENCY WORDS

of

how

make

some

why

animal

Vocabulary Reader

Context Cards

Words to Know

● Read each Context Card.

● Ask a question that uses one of the blue words.

1

of

This bunch of flowers smells sweet.

2

how

How do cats see in the dark?

3 make

She will make a loud sound in music class.

4 some

The boy sees some cows in the field.

5 why

Why do some people like a sour taste?

6 animal

This animal feels soft when the girl pets it.

Background

✓ **WORDS TO KNOW** **Animal Signs**

1. An animal can send a message.

2. How can an animal do that?

3. Some animals move their bodies.

4. Other animals make special sounds.

5. Think of other ways animals communicate.

6. Why not make a list? You will learn a lot!

How Animals Communicate

bird	sings
dog	barks, wags tail
cat	purrs
bee	
wolf	

Comprehension

✓ **TARGET SKILL**   Details

Nonfiction selections are usually about one topic. They have a main idea, or one important idea about the topic. **Details** are facts that tell more about the main idea. Details can give you a clearer picture in your mind about the topic.

As you read **How Animals Communicate**, look for details that tell more about the main idea.

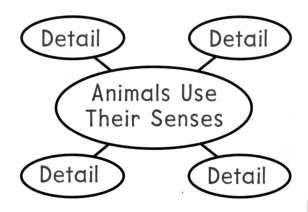

Detail   Detail

Animals Use
Their Senses

Detail   Detail

How Animals Communicate
by William Muñoz

✔ **WORDS TO KNOW**

of	some
how	why
make	animal

✔ **TARGET SKILL**

Details Use details to tell more about the main idea.

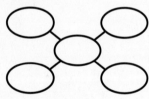

✔ **TARGET STRATEGY**

Infer/Predict Use text clues to figure out important ideas.

GENRE

Informational text gives facts about a topic.

Meet the Author and Photographer

William Muñoz

From the mountains to the prairies, William Muñoz and his camera have traveled all over the United States. He has taken photos of alligators, bald eagles, bison, polar bears, and many other animals in their natural habitats.

How Animals Communicate

written with photographs by William Muñoz

Essential Question

How do animals communicate?

Animals Touch

An animal will tug and grab.

An animal can hug its baby.
How do elephants hug?

The dog and cat are friends.
How can you tell?

What is in the grass?
Animals can hear it.
They will run away from it.

A bird will sing—here I am!

A wolf will call to its pack—here I am!

Animals See

Why will a dog press its legs down?
It will let dogs see—I can play!

Some bees will buzz and dance if they find food.

Animals Smell

A mom can tell the smell of its baby.

An animal can have a bad smell.
It will make animals run away from it!

Touch

Hear

54

See

Smell

Tell what the mom can do.

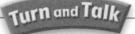

Animal Talk

Write a Caption Draw a picture of two animals communicating. Write a sentence to tell about your picture. Be sure to explain how the animals are communicating.

SCIENCE

Turn and Talk — Senses at Work

Choose one of the senses that animals use to communicate. Talk with a partner about the different ways animals can use that sense. DETAILS

Insect
Messages

Connect to Science

of	some
how	why
make	animal

GENRE
Informational text gives facts about a topic. This is an encyclopedia article.

TEXT FOCUS
Captions tell more information about a photo or picture. Look for captions that label photos.

Insect Messages

An insect is an animal that has six legs. An insect's body has three parts. Most insects have wings so they can fly.

butterfly

Why do insects send messages? Some insects, such as mosquitoes, find each other by flying toward the sound that other mosquitoes' wings make. Honeybees can tell other honeybees where there is food. Every kind of insect has ways of sending messages.

honeybee

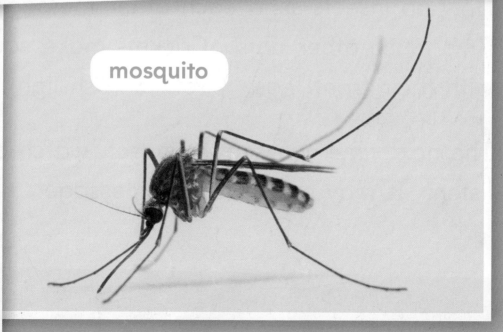

mosquito

ants

How do insects send each other messages?
Ants touch other ants. Crickets make sounds
with their front legs. Fireflies flash light.

The next time you see an insect, watch and
listen. It may be sending a message!

Making Connections

Read Together

 Text to Self

Draw and Label Choose an animal that you like from one of the stories. Draw and label a picture of that animal.

 Text to Text

Discuss What are some ways that insects and other animals communicate?

 Text to World

Connect to Media Discuss with a partner different ways that people communicate.

Grammar

Sentence Parts Every sentence has two parts. The naming part is called the **subject**. The action part is called the **predicate**.

Subject	Predicate
Some cats	play.
Birds	sing softly.
The friends	see the animals.

Read each sentence aloud with a partner. One partner reads the subject and the other reads the predicate. Then switch roles.

1. Bees buzz.

2. A wolf calls.

3. The kittens run away.

4. One mom hugs its baby.

5. Kim hears an elephant.

Grammar in Writing

When you proofread your writing, be sure each sentence has two parts.

Write to Describe

✓ **Word Choice** A poem can describe a thing or explain how the writer feels. It may also have words that rhyme.

Nori wrote a poem about elephants. Then she added details to paint a clearer picture for readers.

Revised Draft

long, gray
Elephants have ∧ trunks

that make a trumpet sound.

Writing Traits Checklist

✓ **Word Choice** Did I choose clear words to describe or explain my topic?

✓ Did I use words that rhyme?

✓ Can I clap a rhythm to my poem?

64

Find details that tell how things look, move, and sound in Nori's poem. Then revise your writing. Use the Checklist.

Final Copy

Elephants

Elephants have

long, gray trunks

that make a trumpet sound.

They use their trunks

to eat and drink

and spray water all around.

Lesson 8

✓ **WORDS TO KNOW**
HIGH-FREQUENCY WORDS

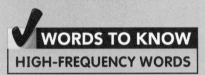

our

today

she

now

her

would

Vocabulary Reader

Context Cards

Words to Know

● Read each Context Card.

● Use a blue word to tell a story about a picture.

1

our

We like to play our games together.

2

today

The music class will practice today.

3 she

She likes to draw with her sister.

4 now

They eat lunch now. Later they will play.

5 her

She took food for her lunch out of the bag.

6 would

Would you like to play with us?

Background Read Together

✔ **WORDS TO KNOW** **Making Music**

1. The concert is today.

2. The teacher will lead our band.

3. She sits at the piano.

4. A girl taps her drum to begin.

5. Now we are ready.

6. Would you like to hear us play?

Would you like to tap a drum like this?
What other music would you like to play?

Comprehension

✓ **TARGET SKILL**   Sequence of Events

The events in a story are often told in an order that is called the **sequence of events.** The sequence of events is what happens **first**, **next**, and **last** in a story.

First   Next   Last

As you read **A Musical Day**, use a chart like this one to tell the order of what happens first, next, and last.

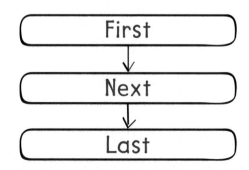

First

↓

Next

↓

Last

JOURNEYS DIGITAL   **Powered by** DESTINATIONReading

Comprehension Activities: Lesson 8

A Musical Day

✔ **WORDS TO KNOW**

our	now
today	her
she	would

✔ **TARGET SKILL**

Sequence of Events
Tell the order in which things happen.

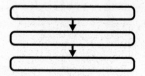

✔ **TARGET STRATEGY**

Analyze/Evaluate Tell how you feel about the text, and why.

GENRE
Realistic fiction is a story that could happen in real life.

Meet the Author

Jerdine Nolen

Some kids collect baseball cards. Others collect shells. When Jerdine Nolen was a kid, she used to collect words. For a long time, **cucumber** was her favorite word. **Plantzilla** and **Raising Dragons** are two books Ms. Nolen has written.

Meet the Illustrator

Frank Morrison

Music and dance have always been part of Frank Morrison's life. He once toured the country as a dancer. The pictures he draws now are so lively they seem like they are dancing!

A Musical Day

written by Jerdine Nolen
illustrated by Frank Morrison

Essential Question

Why is the order of story events important?

Mom and Dad will go on a
trip today.

Our Aunt Viv will be with us.
Tom and I are glad.

We get a big hug from Aunt Viv.
She is lots of fun!

We clap, hop, and sing.

Glen and Meg get here.
Now Aunt Viv has a plan.

She has a big bag.
A lot can fit in her bag.
What is in it?

"Would you kids like to play music?" Aunt Viv said.

"Yes!" we yell.

Meg and I make guitars to pluck.

Tom and Glen make drums to tap.

Tom, Glen, Meg, and I are a band.

It is fun to make music with Aunt Viv!

YourTurn

Working Together

Write Sentences The characters in **A Musical Day** play music together in a band. Write sentences about a time you worked with others to do something fun. Tell what happened first, next, and last.

PERSONAL RESPONSE

Turn and Talk — Making Music

Work with a partner. Talk about how the characters in the story make music. Think about the order of events as you speak.

SEQUENCE OF EVENTS

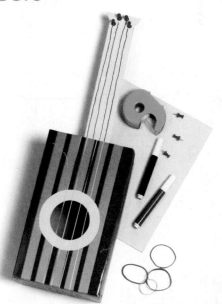

Drums

by **Tim Pano**

People around the world play drums. Yolanda Martinez plays drums. She makes drums, too. She sells her drums.

All drums have a frame. They have a
drumhead, too. Drummers use a beater
stick to play this drum.

Parts of a Drum

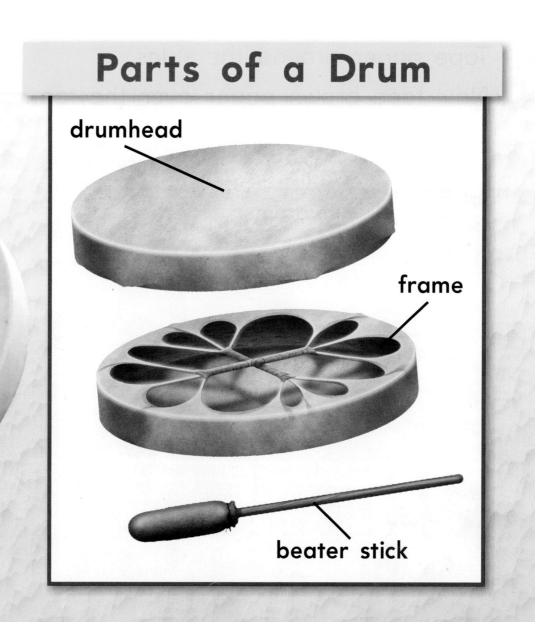

drumhead

frame

beater stick

Make a Drum

Would you like to make a drum today?
Try this.

1 Get an empty coffee can or
an oatmeal carton.

2 Tape paper around the sides.

3 Now tape brown paper over the top.

We like to play our drums.

Making Connections

Read Together

Text to Self

Discuss Music Tell how you like to make music. Speak clearly and slowly so that your classmates understand you.

Text to Text

Connect to Social Studies Use the words and pictures to tell how people in the selections share what they like to do.

Text to World

Write a Note Think about something a family member has taught you. Write a thank-you note to that person. Write details in an order that makes sense.

Grammar

Statements A sentence that tells something is called a **statement**. A statement begins with a capital letter and ends with a period.

The children like to make music.
They play for their class.
One girl taps a drum.

Find the three statements. Write them correctly on another sheet of paper.

1. my friends play in a band

2. sits at his drum set

3. she plucks a guitar

4. the very best singer

5. they have a lot of fun

Grammar in Writing

When you proofread your writing, be sure each statement begins with a capital letter and ends with a period.

Write to Describe

☑ **Word Choice** When you write a **thank-you note**, tell what you are thankful for. Use exact adjectives to make your ideas clear.

Beth wrote a note. Later, she changed **good** to adjectives that are more exact.

Revised Draft

Thank you for the new hat.

It is ~~good~~.
              soft and warm
                    ^

Writing Traits Checklist

☑ **Word Choice** Did I use exact adjectives?

☑ Does my thank-you note have all five parts?

☑ Did I use capital letters and periods correctly?

92

Look for adjectives in Beth's final copy.
Then revise your writing. Use the Checklist.

Final Copy

June 4, 2011

Dear Aunt Jess,

Thank you for the new hat.
It is soft and warm. I really
like the purple stripes.

Love,

Beth

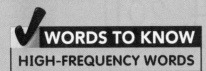

✓ WORDS TO KNOW
HIGH-FREQUENCY WORDS

write

read

pictures

draw

was

after

Vocabulary Reader

Context Cards

Words to Know

- Read each Context Card.
- Use a blue word to tell about something you did.

1

write

They write stories to read in class.

2

read

Dad will read a book to us.

3 pictures

He is looking for some pictures of lions.

4 draw

They all like to draw pictures.

5 was

This animal book was very funny!

6 after

They will go to sleep after the story.

Background

✔ **WORDS TO KNOW** **Making a Book**

1. An author will write a story.

2. An artist gets the story after it is done.

3. The artist will read the story.

4. The artist takes time to draw.

5. The words and pictures are made into a book.

6. This book was fun to read!

paper

pencils

pens

computer

paints

Comprehension

✓ **TARGET SKILL**   Text and Graphic Features

Some nonfiction selections have special
text and features that give them more
information. Special text can be **labels** or
captions. Features can be **photos, graphs,**
or **drawings.**

Dr. Seuss National
Memorial Sculpture
Garden

As you read **Dr. Seuss**, pay attention to the
text and photos. Tell how they are used.

Feature	Purpose

Dr. Seuss
by Helen Lester

✔ **WORDS TO KNOW**

write	draw
read	was
pictures	after

✔ **TARGET SKILL**

Text and Graphic Features Tell how words go with photos.

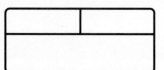

✔ **TARGET STRATEGY**

Question Ask questions about what you are reading.

GENRE

A **biography** tells about events in a person's life.

Meet the Author

Helen Lester

Just like Dr. Seuss, Helen Lester has written a lot of books that make you laugh. She says that the funny characters she creates, such as Tacky the Penguin, are just like the students she had when she was a second-grade teacher.

98

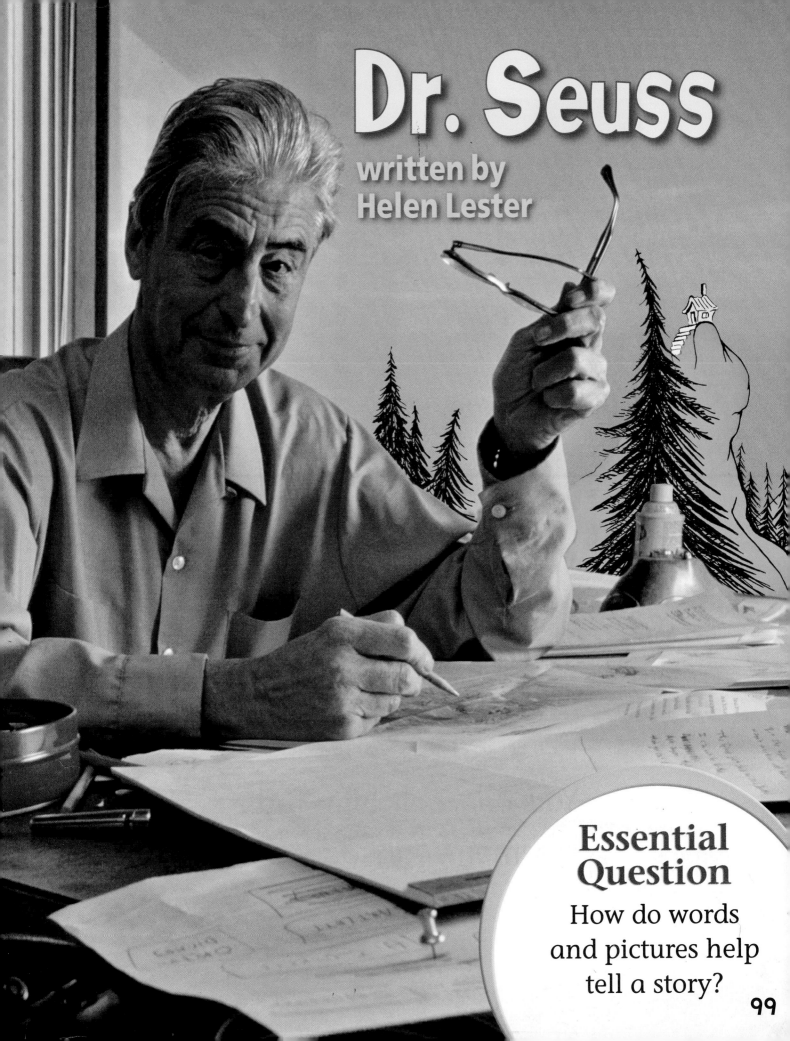

Dr. Seuss

written by
Helen Lester

Essential Question

How do words and pictures help tell a story?

Here is Dr. Seuss.
You can call him Ted.
His mom and dad did!

Ted was a funny man.

Ted would draw pictures.

Here is a fun picture.

Ted would write, too.
Ted wrote **The Cat in the Hat**.

The Cat in the Hat was a big hit!

Can you find **The Cat in the Hat**?

Ted had many big hits after
The Cat in the Hat.

Ted would write rhymes.
Can you find some here?

It was fun to hear Ted read.

Now kids can see animals
from his books.

Dr. Seuss National Memorial
Sculpture Garden

Dr. Seuss is still a big
hit with kids today.

Rhyme Time

Write a Poem Play a rhyming game with a partner. One partner writes a word. The other partner writes a word that rhymes with it. Keep going until you cannot think of more words. Then make up a silly poem that uses the rhyming words. PARTNERS

can

man

fan

Turn and Talk — Picture Talk

Choose one picture from **Dr. Seuss**. Tell a partner how the picture and the words on the page show what Dr. Seuss was like.

TEXT AND GRAPHIC FEATURES

Connect to Poetry

write   draw
read   was
pictures   after

GENRE
Poetry uses the sounds of words to show pictures and feelings.

TEXT FOCUS
Alliteration is a pattern of words with the same beginning sound. Find words that begin with the same sound. How do they make the poems fun to hear and say?

Two Poems from Dr. Seuss

Dr. Seuss liked to write poems. He wrote poems that are fun to read aloud. He would draw pictures to go with them. Dr. Seuss's pictures are as much fun as his poems. After you read these two poems, you might agree that Dr. Seuss was a great writer!

Pete Pats Pigs

Pete Briggs pats pigs.
Briggs pats pink pigs.
Briggs pats big pigs.
(Don't ask me why. It doesn't matter.)
Pete Briggs is a pink pig, big pig patter.

Pete Briggs pats his big pink pigs all day.
(Don't ask me why. I cannot say.)
Then Pete puts his patted pigs away
in his Pete Briggs' Pink Pigs Big Pigs Pigpen.

We have two ducks. One blue. One black.
And when our blue duck goes "Quack-quack"
our black duck quickly quack-quacks back.
The quacks Blue quacks make her quite a quacker
but Black is a quicker quacker-backer.

Write About Sharing

Think about different ways you share. Then
write a poem about sharing. Use pairs of
words that begin with the same sound.

Making Connections

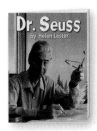

Text to Self

Connect to Language Arts Write a silly poem describing one of your favorite animals. Use rhyming words and words that start with the same sound. Clap the rhythm as you say it.

Text to Text

Express Opinions Look at the pictures in both selections. What do you like best about Dr. Seuss's drawings or poems?

Text to World

Discuss Sharing What special things do you share with your family?

Grammar

Singular and Plural Nouns Some nouns name **one**. Some nouns name **more than one**. An **s** ending means more than one.

One	More Than One
hat	hat**s**

One	More Than One
man	men
woman	women
child	children

Choose the correct noun to name each picture. Take turns with a partner. Tell why you chose a noun that names one or more than one.

1. book   books

2. stamp   stamps

3. man   men

4. cat   cats

5. child   children

Grammar in Writing

Write the correct noun to name each picture. Use another sheet of paper.

Write to Describe (Read Together)

☑ **Ideas** Before you start writing, plan the details for your **description**. A friend can help by asking you questions.

Josh asked Evan about **The Cat in the Hat**.

Does the cat have a tail? How do his feet look?

Exploring a Topic

Prewriting Checklist

 Did I choose a topic I know a lot about?

 Do my details tell how the character looks?

 Did I write adjectives for size, shape, color, and number?

Look for details in Evan's plan. Then plan your own description. Use the Checklist.

Planning Chart

Head
tall hat
red and white

Body
long, thin tail

My Topic
cat

Arms
white gloves

Legs
two furry feet

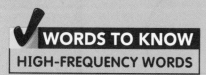

✓ **WORDS TO KNOW**

HIGH-FREQUENCY WORDS

give

one

small

put

eat

take

Vocabulary
Reader

Context
Cards

122

Words to Know

Read Together

- Read each Context Card.

- Choose two blue words.
  Use them in sentences.

1

give

She will give a gift to her friend.

2

one

There was one cupcake on the plate.

3 small

The **small** red box is on the left.

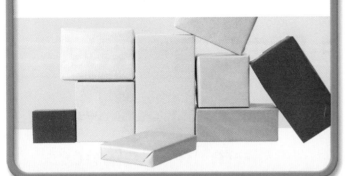

4 put

They **put** the party hats on their heads.

5 eat

The children **eat** pizza at the party.

6 take

They both **take** some balloons home.

Background

✔ **WORDS TO KNOW** **Time for a Party!**

1. Bake **one** big cake.

2. **Put** candles on top.

3. Place **small** dishes on the table.

4. **Give** each person a fork.

5. **Take** a slice of cake.

6. **Eat** and enjoy!

A Party Checklist

✔ Make a list of friends.

✔ Ask the friends to come.

✔ Get ready.

✔ Bake a cake.

Have fun!

Comprehension

✔ **TARGET SKILL** Story Structure

A story has different parts. The **characters** are the people and animals in a story. The **setting** is when and where a story takes place. The **plot** is the order of events that tells about a problem in the story and how the characters solve it.

As you read **A Cupcake Party**, use a story map to tell who is in the story, where they are, and what they do.

Character	Setting
Plot	

Comprehension Activities: Lesson 10

Main Selection

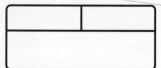
Meet the Author and Illustrator

David McPhail

David McPhail wanted to be a baseball player when he was growing up, but he wasn't good at sports. Next, Mr. McPhail wanted to play guitar in a band. Finally, he went to art school. He was great at drawing pictures and writing stories!

A Cupcake Party

written and illustrated by
David McPhail

**Essential
Question**

How do the parts
of a story work
together?

127

"I miss my friends," Fritz said.
"I must have a big party!"

Fritz had a list of friends to
ask to his party.

Fritz went to ask Kit.

"I will come," Kit said.

"It will be grand!"

Fritz went to ask Jack next.

Jack said yes.

"A party is fun!" Jack said.

Fritz met Fran and Stan at a
tree stump.
Fran and Stan said yes, too.

Fritz went to ask Glen last.
"I will not miss it," Glen said.

Fritz baked cupcakes to
give to his friends.

He put a small picture
on every one.

Fritz felt glad to see his friends.

"Take the cupcake with a picture
of you on it," Fritz said.

His friends had a snack
for Fritz, too.

139

"Yum! Now we can eat
and have fun," Fritz said.

Your Turn

Thank You, Fritz!

Make a Card Make a thank-you card for Fritz from one of his friends who came to the party. Write sentences that tell why the party was fun.

LANGUAGE ARTS

Turn and Talk — Fritz and Friends

Work with a partner. Make a list of all the characters in **A Cupcake Party**. Tell what each character does in the story.

STORY STRUCTURE

Connect to Math

✔ **WORDS TO KNOW**

give	put
one	eat
small	take

GENRE

Readers' theater is a text that has been written for readers to read aloud.

TEXT FOCUS

Directions tell how to do something step-by-step. Follow the directions on page 144 with an adult to make a tasty treat!

Readers' Theater

At the Bakery

by Kim Lee

Cast of Characters

 Baker

 Helper 1

 Helper 2

 What have you baked today, Baker?

 I baked cupcakes. Can you help me?

I can help you eat the cupcakes!

 No, no! The cupcakes are not finished yet.

 How can we help?

 You can put the frosting on top. I will give you the recipe.

 Then we can eat the cupcakes!

Here is a baker's recipe
for real frosting.

Frosting Recipe

4 cups powdered sugar

4 tablespoons milk

$\frac{1}{2}$ cup butter, softened

2 teaspoons vanilla extract

- Put all the ingredients in a large bowl.

- Take a mixer and beat at low speed for one minute until the frosting is creamy.

- Spread a small amount on each cupcake.

Making Connections

Text to Self

Make a List Pretend you are having a party. Make a list of foods you would make for your guests.

Text to Text

Connect to Social Studies How did the characters in each story help each other?

Text to World

Write Sentences Write sentences to tell how you could help a neighbor or a family member bake cupcakes.

Grammar

Prepositions A **preposition** is a word that joins with other words to help tell where something is or when it happens. A **prepositional phrase** is a group of words that starts with a preposition.

Prepositions for Where

Where are the leaves?	The leaves are **on** the ground.
Where is the chipmunk?	The chipmunk ran **up** the tree.
Where are the birds?	The birds are **in** the nest.

Prepositions for When

When did you take a walk?	I took a walk **before** lunch.
When did you eat lunch?	I ate lunch **after** the walk.
What time did you eat?	I ate lunch **at** noon.

Find the preposition in each sentence.
Write it on a sheet of paper. Talk with a
partner. Decide if the preposition tells
where something is or when it happened.

1. I saw a chipmunk on a branch.

2. We watched the stars after dinner.

3. My brother climbed up a tree.

4. We went home before dark.

5. Pretty flowers grow in the woods.

Grammar in Writing

When you revise your writing, look for
places where you can use a preposition.

Write to Describe

Read Together

✔ **Organization** A good **description** begins with a topic sentence that tells what the description is about.

Evan wrote a draft of his description. Then he added a topic sentence.

Revised Draft

The cat looks very funny.
∧His tall hat is red and white.

Revising Checklist

✔ Did I write a topic sentence?

✔ Could I add any prepositions?

✔ Did I spell my words correctly?

Look for adjectives in Evan's final copy.
Then revise your writing. Use the Checklist.

Final Copy

The Cat in the Hat

The cat looks very funny.

His tall hat is red and white.

The cat wears white gloves.

He has a long, thin tail
and two furry feet.

Read Together

Read the next two stories. Then tell the order of events in each story.

Come and Get It!

Mom makes the best pancakes. I can help her make some for my friends. First, I get a big bowl. Next, I put in the eggs. I crack them one by one. I take a fork and beat them. Then, I mix in a cup of milk.

Mom puts more in the bowl. I mix it up. Next, Mom gets a pan. We let it get hot. Mom helps me put the mix in the pan. She lets me flip the pancakes. I yell to my friends, "Come and get it!"

The pancakes are good. We eat them all.

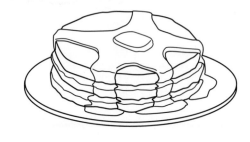

The Mix-Up

Jan and Dad make cookies. Jan puts the mix on a cookie pan. Dad puts the pan in the oven.

Dad takes out the hot cookies. Then Jan and Dad pick cookies to eat. "Yuck!" they yell. "Our cookies are not very good!"

Then Dad grins. He looks at a bag they put in the mix. "This bag does not have sugar in it. This bag has salt!" It was a big, bag mix-up!

Unit 2 Wrap-Up

The Big Idea

Share with a Friend Think of a time when you shared something with a friend. Draw a picture and write a sentence to tell what you shared.

I shared my cheese sandwich with Patty.

Listening and Speaking

Box Music Use an empty shoe box and rubber bands to make a guitar. Stretch rubber bands around the box. Pluck the rubber bands to make a song. Then share it with friends.

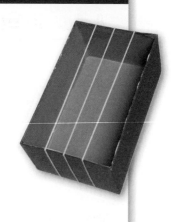

Words to Know

Unit 2 High-Frequency Words

6 Jack and the Wolf
come
said
call
hear
away
every

7 How Animals Communicate
of
how
make
some
why
animal

8 A Musical Day
our
today
she
now
her
would

9 Dr. Seuss
write
read
pictures
draw
was
after

10 A Cupcake Party
give
one
small
put
eat
take

Glossary

A

aunt

Your **aunt** is the sister of your mother or your father.
I have one **aunt** on my father's side of the family.

B

baby

A **baby** is a very young child.
Tonya's family has a new
little **baby**.

baked

To **bake** is to cook in the oven.
My dad and I **baked** a cake for Mom's birthday.

band

A **band** is a group of people who play music together.
My brother plays drums in a **band**.

bees

A **bee** is an insect that can fly. The **bees** were buzzing around the flower.

bird

A **bird** is an animal with wings and feathers. Danny watched the **bird** fly away from the nest.

books

A **book** is a group of pages with words on them. We read **books** all the time at home.

C

cupcakes

A **cupcake** is a small, round cake. We ate **cupcakes** at Jenna's birthday party.

D

dance

To **dance** means to move your body to music. That song always makes me want to **dance**.

down

Down means going from a high place to a low place. She looked **down** from the top floor.

Dr.

Dr. is a short way to write **Doctor**. Our family goes to **Dr.** Lopez when we are sick.

E

elephants

An **elephant** is a very big animal with a long trunk. We saw five **elephants** at the zoo.

F

food

Food is what people or animals eat.
My favorite **food** is pasta.

G

guitars

A **guitar** is a musical
instrument. There are
two **guitars** in our band.

H

head

Your face and your ears are part of your **head**. That tall
man's **head** is blocking the picture.

hit

A **hit** is something that many people like. That song
was a **hit** with all the kids.

M

music

Music is sounds people make with instruments and their voices. My dad and I like to play folk **music**.

O

once upon a time

Once upon a time is a storytelling phrase that means long ago. Many stories begin with the words **once upon a time**.

P

party

A **party** is a time when people get together to have fun. I am going to have a **party** on my birthday.

R

rhymes

A **rhyme** is made up of words that have the same sound at the end. We say **rhymes** when we jump rope.

S

sheep
A **sheep** is an animal covered with wool.
The **sheep** were eating grass on the hill.

smell
A **smell** is something that you sense with your nose.
The skunk left a very strong **smell**.

T

tree
A **tree** is a kind of plant with branches and leaves. We have a huge **tree** in our front yard.

trick
To **trick** is to get people to do something they do not want to do. She tried to **trick** us into giving her our lunch money.

W

wolf

A **wolf** is a wild animal that looks like a dog. The **wolf** watched the sheep very carefully.

wrote

Wrote means to write in the past. Tía Sofía **wrote** me a letter last week.

Acknowledgments

"Pete Pats Pigs" from *Oh Say Can You Say?* by Dr. Seuss. TM & © by Dr. Seuss Enterprises, L.P. 1979. Reprinted by permission of Random House Children's Books, a division of Random House, Inc., and International Creative Management.

"We have two ducks…" from *Oh Say Can You Say?* by Dr. Seuss. TM & © by Dr. Seuss Enterprises, L.P. 1979. Reprinted by permission of Random House Children's Books, a division of Random House, Inc., and International Creative Management.

Credits

Photo Credits

Placement Key: (t) top; (b) bottom; (l) left; (r) right; (c) center; (bkgd) background; (frgd) foreground; (i) inset.

TOC **8a** full (c)George Doyle/Getty Images; **8b** spread (c)BlendImages/Tips Images; **9** (c)HMCo; **10** (t) (c)Arco Images/Wittek R./Alamy; (b) (c) Wolfgang Kaehler/Corbis; **11** (tl) (c)Gerry Ellis/ Minden Pictures; (tr) (c)Tim Pannell/Corbis; (bl) (c)Daniel J. Cox/Photographer's Choice/Getty Images; (br) (c)Jeffrey Lepore/Photo Researchers, Inc.; **12** (c)Neil Beckerman/Riser/Getty Images; **14** (c)Courtesty of Chris Sheban; **35** (cr) (c)Kurt Banks/Alamy; **38** (t) (c)Alex Mares-Manton/Asia Images/Getty Images; **38** (b) (c)Ingo Bartussek/ Naturepl.com; **39** (tl) (c)Image84/Alamy ; (tr) (c) David De Lossy/Photodisc/Getty Images; (bl) (c)Michael Newman/PhotoEdit; (br) (c)Rhoda Sidney/PhotoEdit; (c)Cynthia Diane Pringle/ CORBIS; (c)Tom Brakefield/CORBIS; (c)Robert W. Ginn/PhotoEdit; (c)LMR Group/Alamy; **41** (tr) (c)Arthur Morris/Corbis; **42** c) (c)William Munoz; **43** spread (c)William Munoz; **44** (c (c) William Munoz; **45** (c (c)Keith Szafranski; **54** (c (c)Visual&Written SL/Alamy; **47** (c (c)W. Perry Conway/CORBIS; **48** (c (c)Steve & Dave Maslowski/Photo Researchers Inc.; **49** (c (c) William Munoz; **50** (c (c)Francois Goheir/Photo Researchers, Inc.; **51** (c (c)Scott Camazine/Alamy; **52** (c (c)William Munoz; **53** (c (c)Keith Szafranski; **54** (t) (c)William Munoz; **54** (b) (c)Steve & Dave Maslowski/Photo Researchers Inc.; **55** (t) (c) Francois Goheir/Photo Researchers, Inc.; **55** (b) (c)William Munoz; **56** c) (c)William Munoz Photography; **58** (b) (c)Gary Vestal/Getty Images; **59** (b) (c)Frank Greenaway/Getty Images; **59** (t) (c)Martin Rugner/AGE Fotostock;